HOW TO ACHIEVE
COLOR ACCURACY
IN YOUR PHOTOGRAPHS:

USE CUSTOM WHITE BALANCING

BOB REWICK

I. INTRODUCTION

This book is about matching the colors of subjects you see in the real world with the colors you record for them on your camera. Quite often, the colors in your photographs are not the same as you originally saw them.

Most photographers are aware that their cameras must be adjusted to match the lighting under which their images are taken, by a camera feature known as white balancing (WB).

Quite frequently, however, none of the available WB settings will adjust a photograph to its original colors, even though you may think you have correctly identified the lighting conditions.

But, most lighting sources are not monochromatic, that is, they consist of a variety of wavelengths and colors. How then could any single WB setting, or a variety of 5 or six settings, be able to match such common mixed lighting sources?

Photoshop to the rescue? Perhaps in some cases, yes, but there is a WB setting called custom white balancing (CWB) that few of us use because it seems too complicated and camera instruction manuals often poorly explain.

Wouldn't it be better to adjust the camera to the true lighting conditions while still in the "field", before trying to remember the colors later on a computer? This is the process I wish the reader understand by using CWB.

You may say that exact color matching is not a great concern for you because the viewers of your photographs were not there to check the accuracy of your color tones. And, you can later adjust the color balance of nearly every photograph on a computer.

But, what if you wish to record the accurate colors of a new plant or animal species, or advertise food, jewelry, or other commercial items? Many consumers might be dismayed to find the colors of items they purchase to be different from how they saw them in ads.

II. BACKGROUND

Camera exposure adjustments have little to do with the colors we see. For example, a red stop sign and a gray tree branch both reflect about 18% of the light shining on them, but are obviously different colors.

Exposure variations only lighten or darken colors, without generally affecting their basic tones--red is still red, perhaps only muted or brighter--but red cannot be converted to blue unless there is a lighting change.

Although our eyes are extremely more sensitive to colors than a camera, our brains usually view familiar subjects the way we expect to see them, independent of the lighting source. Thus, we are often subconsciously unaware of small color shifts that a camera will easily detect.

Many photographers depend heavily on the camera's WB controls to adjust the color balance in their photographs to the lighting conditions around them.

However, few camera manuals and literature references inform the photographer that: (a) WB settings are only approximations to the real lighting conditions, (b) nearly every photographic location is illuminated by mixed lighting, and (c) CWB can provide a first-step solution to most color miss-matches.

In this book, I will:

    A. Provide a brief review of color.

    B. Define white balance.

    C. Discuss the ever-presence of mixed lighting.

    D. Describe how mixed lighting will affect the color balance of a photograph.

    E. Explain custom white balancing (CWB).

    F. Show a schematic drawing of the CWB process.

    G. Present clear operating instructions for using CWB.

    H. Show photographs that have been color-corrected by CWB under a difficult mixed lighting situation.

III. COLOR

We live in a world of color, not because the subjects themselves are colored, but due to their interaction with light. Living and innate objects have no inherent color. They extract colors from the radiation that shines upon them. Thus, color doesn't exist without light.

The process that gives us a colored world is absorption and reflection. Many materials absorb selective colors from sunlight and other sources, and then reflect the non-absorbed portion.

Thus, an apple appears red because the green and blue portions of white light have been absorbed, and the only color left, red, is reflected.

But, all lighting sources have a different color spectrum, and a specific wavelength may not be present for the subject to absorb. For example, a banana will not appear yellow under fluorescent or tungsten lighting because the color (s) a banana wants to absorb is (are) missing or reduced.

Usually our brains compensate for lighting differences, and still see the banana as yellow, but film and digital sensors cannot make this adjustment.

IV. WHITE BALANCE

White balance (WB) is the process for restoring the colors of subjects you see under different lighting conditions to how you would expect to see them in daylight.

Many photographers are told that the only way to achieve color accuracy in your photographs is to adjust your white balance control knob to match the color of the light that is striking your subject.

WB can be expressed in terms of the color temperature of the light, such as about 5400 degrees K for sunlight, and about 3400 degrees K for tungsten.   These numbers are not the actual temperature of the light, but are equivalent to the color of a flame as it is heated.

Degrees K is a temperature scale that differs from the degrees C scale by about 273. Thus, 100 degrees C = 373 degrees K.

For example, when you view a log in the fireplace, the first color you see is red, and then as the fire gets hotter, the color transitions through blue into white. Thus, photographically speaking, red has a cooler color temperature than blue.

Some photographers confuse exposure with color. They may believe that once the proper exposure has been achieved (by gray card reference, or HDR), the colors will be correct, too.

However, exposure and color balance are not always related. Remember, green grass, brown tree trunks and a red stop sign are equally 18 % reflective, but are obviously different colors.

The major reasons why WB balance control settings are not always effective for every lighting condition are: (1) the settings are only mid-range approximations of the actual lighting source, and (2) the settings do not adequately deal with mixed lighting illumination.

For example, "daylight" can change over 5,000 degrees K from dawn to dusk. The common WB selections cannot correct such lighting disparities, and the colors you photograph will vary.

V. LIGHTING

The lighting that strikes your subject is rarely uniform. It usually comes from a variety of sources: sunny, shade, shadow, fluorescent, tungsten, etc., which I call "mixed lighting".

Although most photographers recognize individual lighting sources, mixed lighting is subtler and frequently difficult to detect.

Mixed lighting is a major problem for studio photographers who wish to create accurate color renditions of their subjects. They frequently have to calibrate their strobes to insure consistent light output as the bulbs and tubes age.

Most photographers don't blame mixed lighting for color shifts in their prints. They more commonly suggest the problem lies with their cameras, lenses, computers, and printers.

VI. CUSTOM WHITE BALANCING

Custom White Balancing is the process of referencing the incident lighting striking a subject against a subject's colors that have been shifted from the effects of mixed lighting.

The camera uses the reference information to correct the shifted colors to how you should see them initially under daylight.

Few photographers realize that CWB is more sensitive to lighting differences than any other WB setting on your camera, including AWB. CWB deals with the largest range of color temperatures you will probably encounter: from about 2,000 degrees K to about 10,000 degrees K.

Thus, CWB has the potential for correcting extreme color disparity problems.

VII. SCHEMATIC OF THE CWB PROCESS

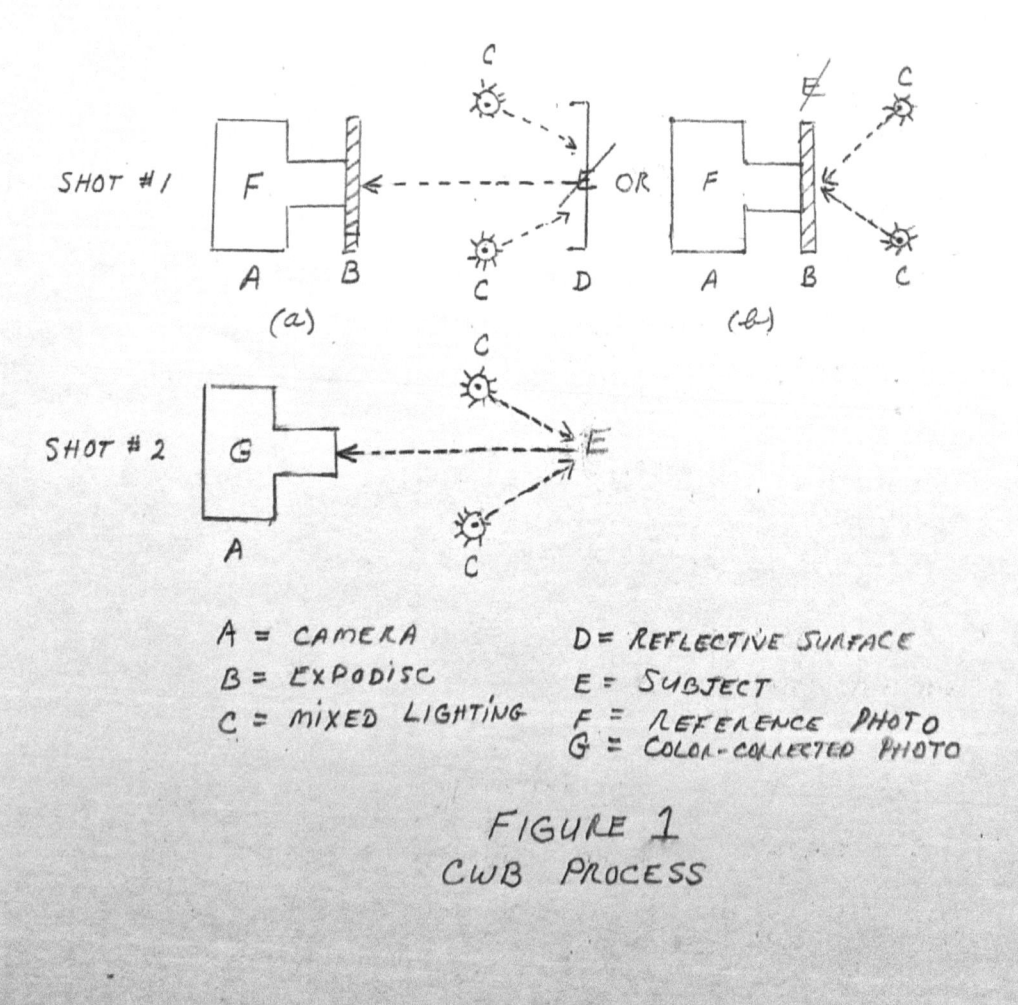

A = CAMERA   D = REFLECTIVE SURFACE
B = EXPODISC   E = SUBJECT
C = MIXED LIGHTING F = REFERENCE PHOTO
                  G = COLOR-CORRECTED PHOTO

FIGURE 1
CWB PROCESS

The Custom White Balancing procedure simply involves taking two photographs: the first, a reference shot of the lighting, and the second, the subject.

I summarize the CWB procedure below:

1. Take Shot 1(a) or Shot 1(b) in Figure1 with the ExpoDisc filter (B) to obtain a reference image (F) of the incident light striking the subject, without the subject in the scene.

2. I show the absence of subject (E) in Shots 1(a) and 1(b) by drawing a line through the letter E.

3. If you cannot face the incident lighting, photograph a highly reflective white card or metallic foil in the same position as the subject, Shot 1(a)

4. Use the camera's control knobs to store the reference image from Shot 1(a) or (b) (F) into the camera's memory (G).

5. Take Shot 2 to obtain an image of the subject in the scene, with filter (B) removed.

The CWB procedure will, of course, differ among camera models, but the steps are usually similar. However, few instructions mention the use of an ExpoDisc filter.

If you have a Canon DSLR or point-and shoot (I use a Canon 7D), I can send you CWB operating instructions. Just ask me for my email address.

VIII. THE EXPODISC

The ExpoDisc is used to take the CWB reference photograph (see Figure 1).

The ExpoDisc resembles an ordinary filter, such as a polarizer or neutral density filter, except that it has a variegated front surface. It screws into a camera lens, but is only available in a 77-mm thread size. However, this filter can be held in front of lenses with smaller thread sizes while you are taking the reference photograph.

You may be concerned about where to point the ExpoDisc when you are using it for the reference information. The Disc must face the incoming light. But, this is not easily accomplished, especially when the lighting is coming from different angles.

To compensate for difficult shooting locations, I place an incident light reflector, such as a white card or an aluminum foil, at the same spot as the subject. Thus, when I use the ExpoDisc to photograph the reflector, my exposure should be nearly equivalent to the incident lighting.

You may then ask me another question: "What if I can't easily walk up to my subject and cover it with a white card, such as in a distant scenic?" My answer: select the most highly reflective subject in your scene, preferably nearly white or metallic, and use that for your reference CWB photograph.

However, this approach may be difficult to achieve, because you must fill the entire CWB viewing area with the bright subject, and avoid the presence of less reflective nearby subjects.

For example, if your reference photograph includes a gray subject (grass, brown tree limbs, a red stop sign, etc.) in the scene, you may get the wrong answer. Gray tones reflect only about 18% of the incident lighting, not the 100% you want.

The photo I show below is a typical reference image of the incident lighting. As you can see, it is featureless and reddish in color, probably due to the mixed lighting ratios I used.

IX. CWB PHOTOGRAPHS

Next, I show three subjects I photographed under an artificial lighting mixture (60% daylight, 30% fluorescent, and 10% tungsten). As you can see, the subject's colors are harsher than you would expect.

Before using CWB, I examined the shifted colors using the standard WB control knobs on the camera. As I observed on "live view", no setting fully restored the colors of these subjects to how I viewed them under daylight shade lighting.

The subjects were photographed under the following conditions:

A. Lighting

    (a). diffuse window daylight (60%).

    (b). a CFL fluorescent bulb (30%).

    (c). a 60-W tungsten bulb (10%).

    The percentage contribution of each lighting source is only an approximation.

B. Camera

    (a). Canon 7D DSLR mounted on a tripod.

    (b). Canon 10-22 mm wide-angle lens.

    (c). Focal length about 15-mm.

(d). Aperture = f/29.

(e). Exposure time about 2.5 seconds.

Subject # 1: Photograph Before CWB

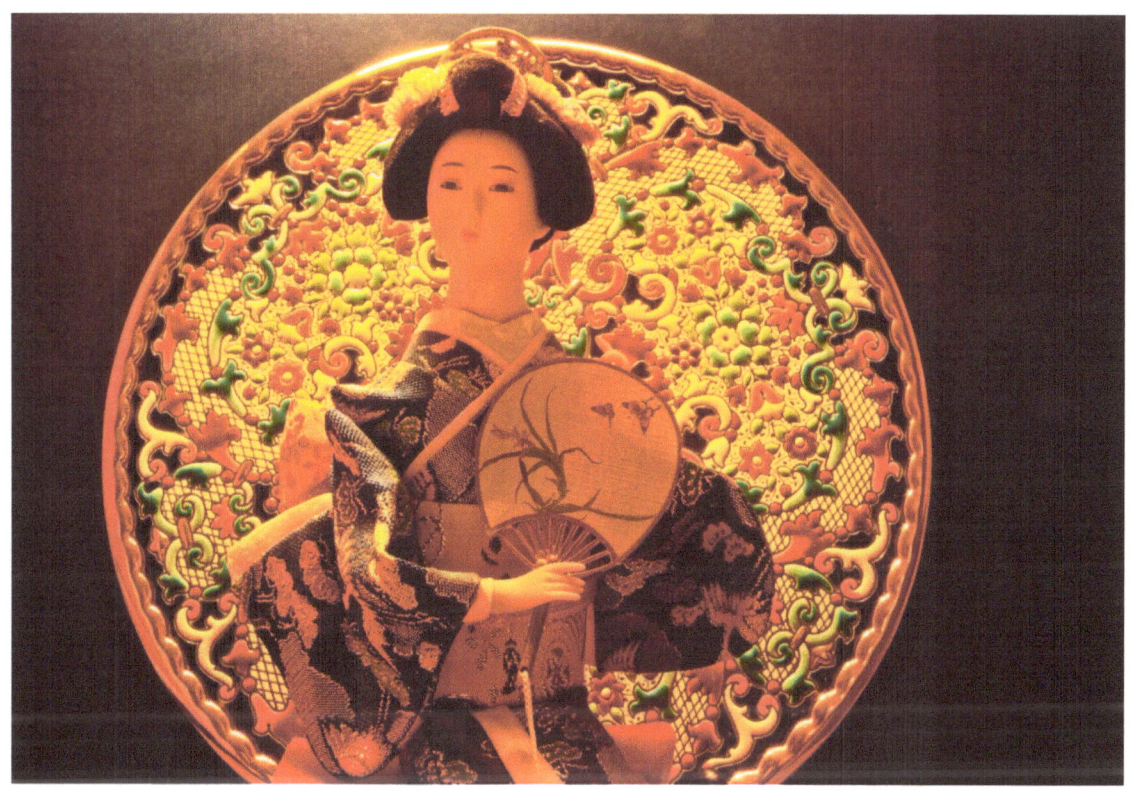

Subject # 1: Photograph After CWB

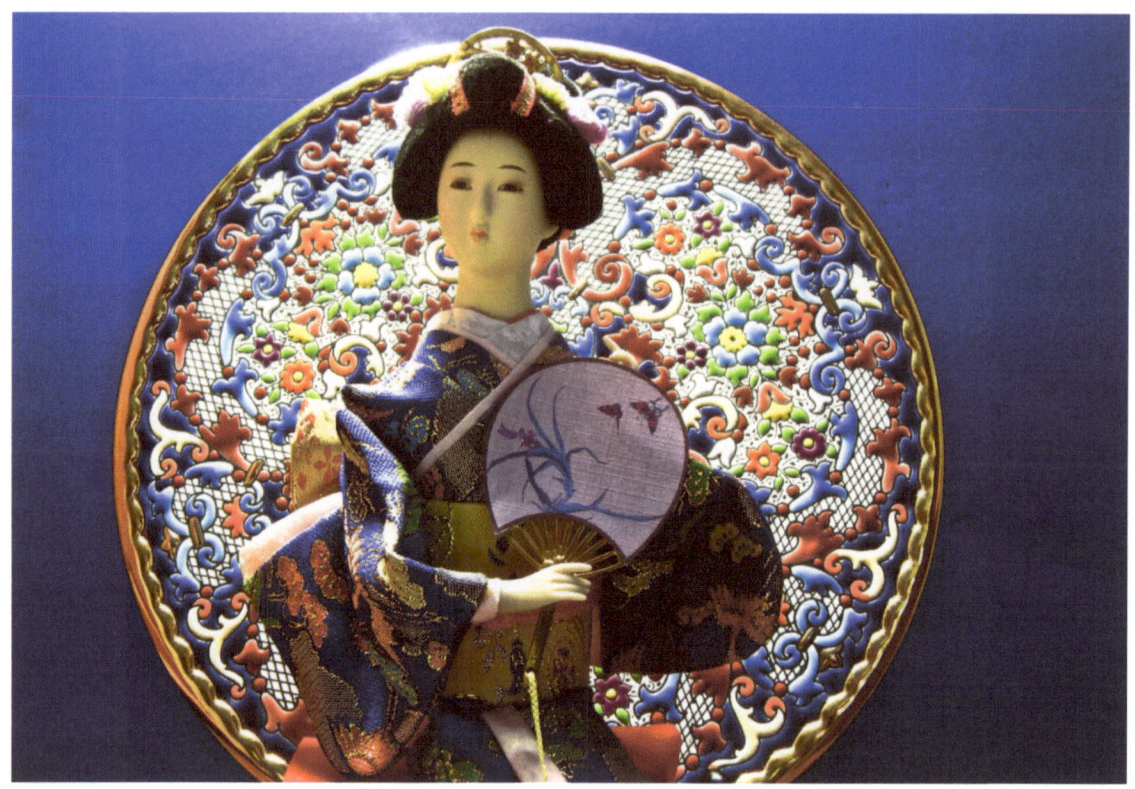

Subject # 2: Photograph Before CWB

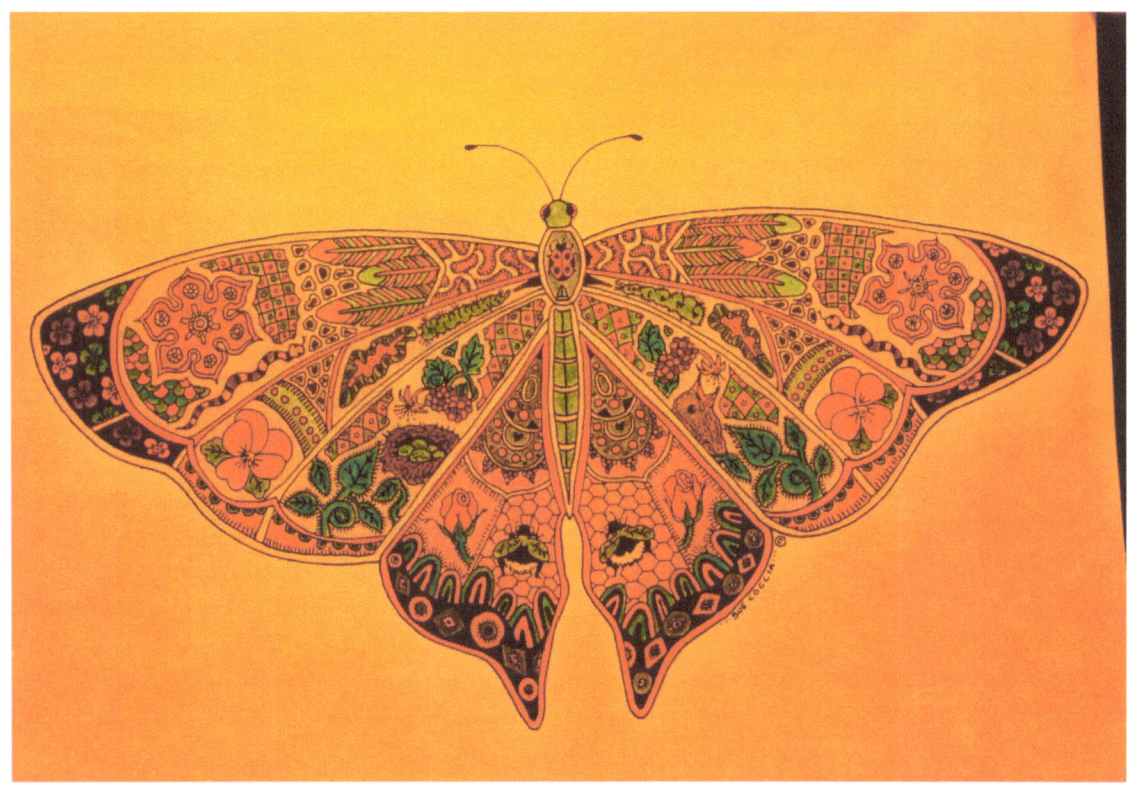

Subject # 2: Photograph After CWB

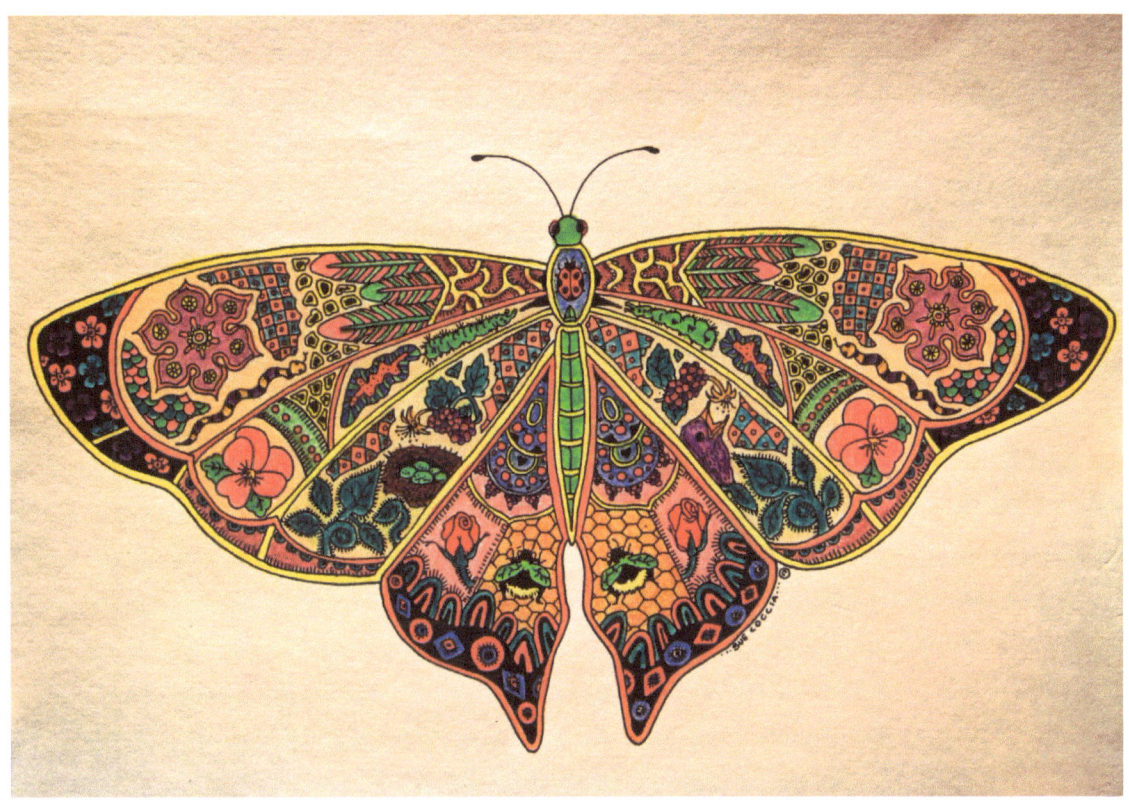

Subject # 3: Photograph Before CWB

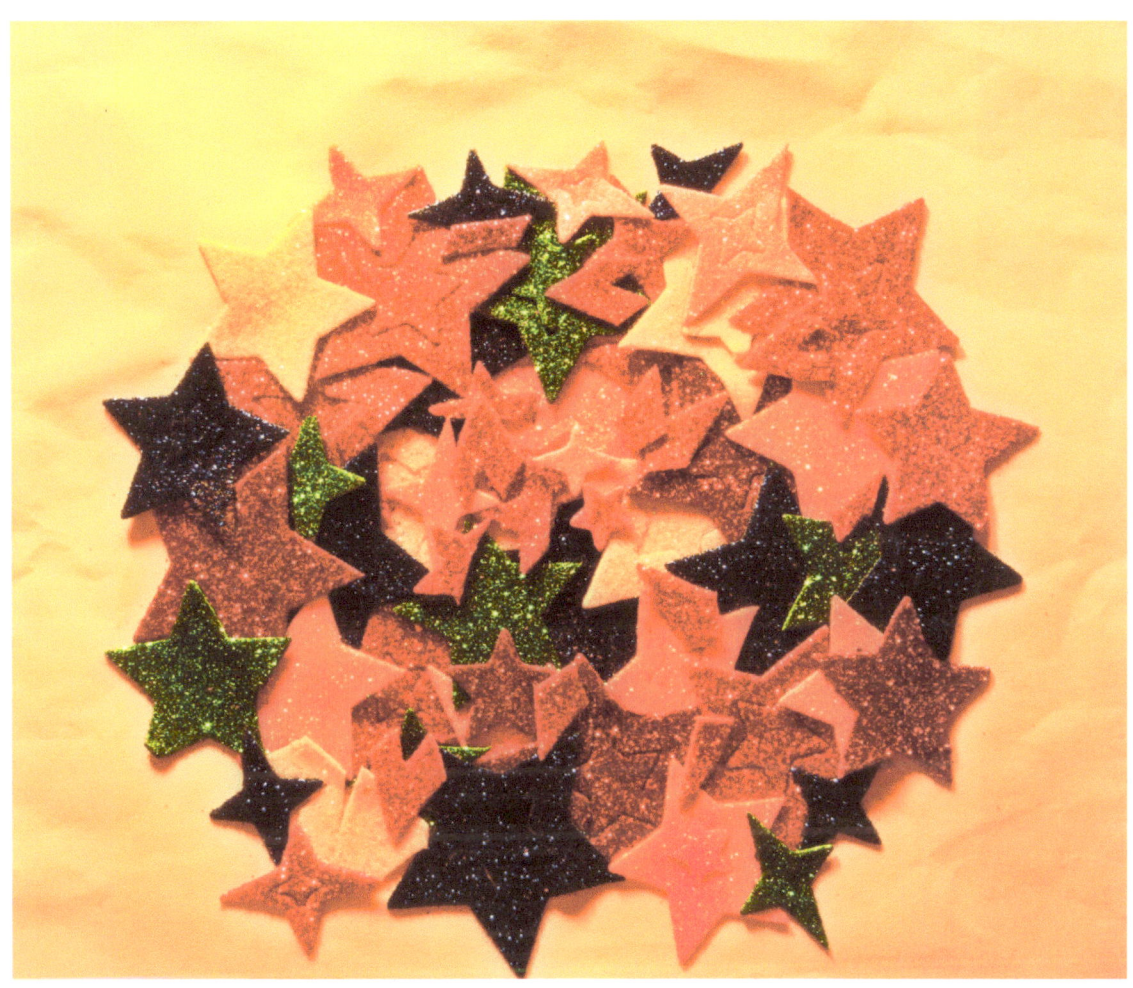

Subject # 3: Photograph After CWB

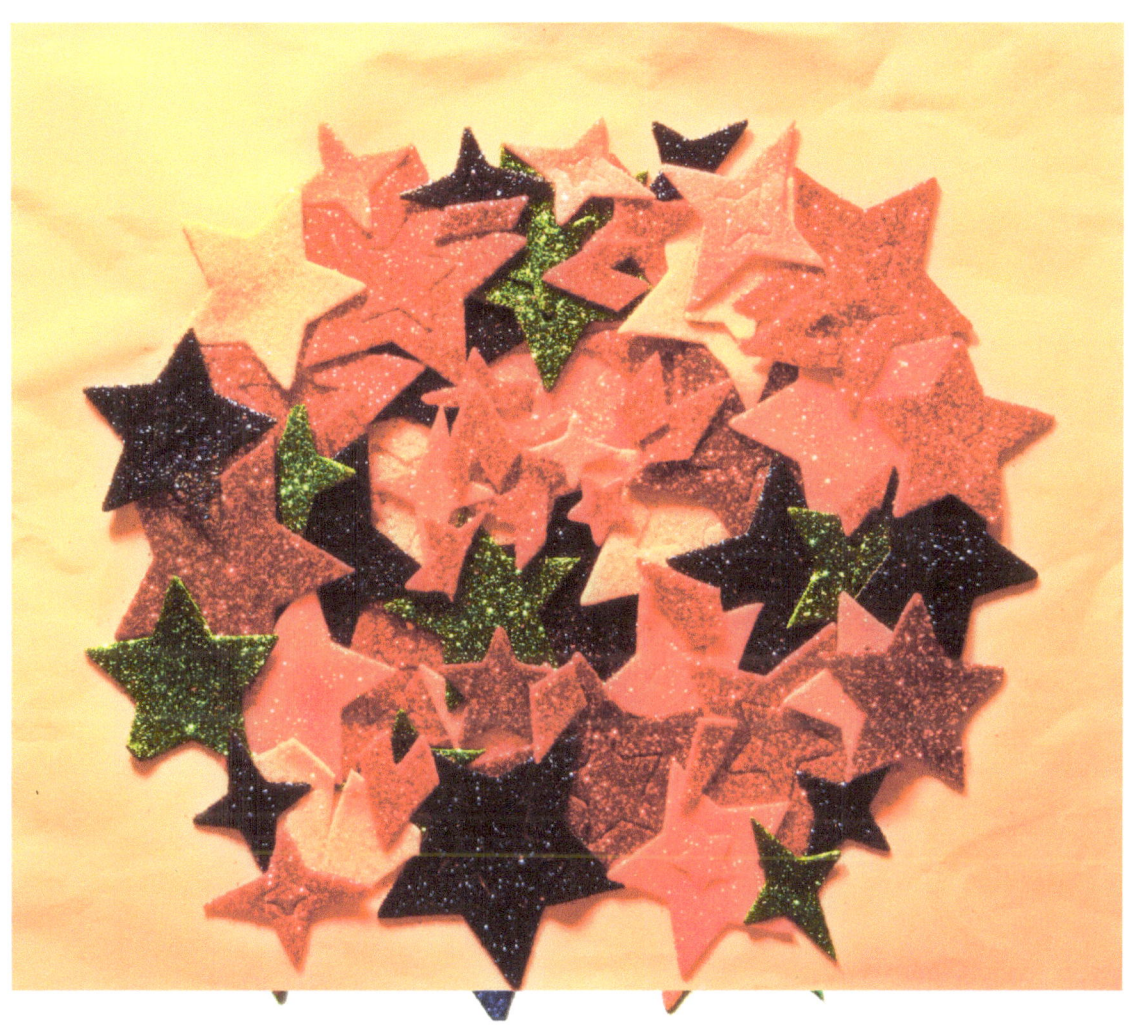

X. RESULTS

From the above **Photographs**, you can clearly observe significant color changes between the "before" and "after" CWB shots.

Remember, the "before" CWB shot was taken under the mixed lighting condition I chose to investigate (about 60 % daylight, 30 % fluorescent, and 10 % tungsten).

An accurate comparison between the "after" CWB photograph and its original color under monochromatic lighting is difficult to assess, because I did not record an initial photograph.

However, I can subjectively report that the garish-colored mixed lighting photographs, "before CWB", were not close to how I saw the subjects originally.

XI. SUMMARY AND CONCLUSIONS

I believe my results show that you can dramatically improve the color fidelity of your photographs taken under mixed lighting conditions, and probably in situations where you don't even suspect that diverse lighting is present.

I propose you use CWB for all the important photographs you take--especially those you can't easily repeat.

However, I know that some of you may prefer to use a computer color-editing program; if one exists that modifies only selective color tones and not all the others. By viewing the histogram in i-photo, the editing program I use, I see a continuous shift of all colors.

In many cases, I prefer to color edit (CWB) my images in the camera before subjecting them to computer attack. Resolution loss is always a bi-product of cyber editing. And, by the time I do get to a computer, I usually have forgotten what the original colors of my subjects were.

Moreover, the time I can save by using CWB instead of a computer might be compensated by more time I can spend in the field taking photographs, rather than sitting in front of a glaring computer screen.

So, give CWB a try. I think you will find the method to be a valuable on-camera color-editing technique. The only extra equipment you need to carry with you is an ExpoDisc filter and a white card.

XII. ABOUT THE AUTHOR

Bob Rewick is a professional photographer, a teacher, and a research physical-inorganic chemist, surface scientist, and spectroscopist. He worked at SRI International, Menlo Park, CA, for 32 years, and 3D Technology Labs for 8 years, where he specialized in the optical properties of materials such as semiconductors and up-converting phosphors.

Bob began his photography career in about 1985 by taking many classes, workshops, and seminars from well-known photographers, and at local colleges. He currently belongs to 2 local camera clubs.
He has displayed his work at several San Francisco Bay Area gallery locations.

Bob has travelled extensively around world and the U.S., and has published many photography articles and several books (about 15).

He serves as a photography judge at local camera club competitions, teaches private individuals, and lectures on a wide variety of photography subjects.

Bob, and his wife Joy, are co-owners of "Photo Expressions", a business concerned with teaching the "art" of photography, and learning how to "see".

To view some of Bob's very early photographs (probably about 13 years ago) in a preliminary website, Google the names Joy and Bob Rewick on the Internet. Some of his more recent work can be seen in his more than 25 photography publications in national journals and on the Internet. A more current website is under development.

For questions, comments, or for more information concerning this book, please contact Bob at: jbrewick@earthlink.net.